To Dad

From

_____

On this date

_____

Thanks, Dad!

~In Appreciation of All You Do~

Jennifer Hahn

LIFE AFFORDS NO GREATER RESPONSIBILITY, NO
GREATER PRIVILEGE,
THAN THE RAISING
OF THE NEXT GENERATION.

C. EVERETT KOOP

A father is defined as "a man who has begotten a child."
But a dad is so much more. He is a playmate, encourager,
teacher, counselor, and friend. As children, we rarely express
to our dads exactly how much we appreciate them.
This book, which includes scripture, quotations, stories,
and letters from a maturing child's point of view,
is meant as a tribute to those men whom we proudly
call "DADDY."

Although we cannot fully express our gratitude
for all you have done, we do say,

Thanks, Dad!
—for everything

Train a child in the way he should go, and when he is old he will not turn from it.

PROVERBS 22:6 NIV

Now it is required that those who have been given a trust must prove faithful.

1 CORINTHIANS 4:2 NIV

Dear Daddy,

Today I entered the world, and how different it is from where I was before. I had felt so safe and warm; then that changed so very quickly. But when I felt you take me in your arms, I had a wonderful new feeling of security. I heard your voice and knew you were the man who would hold that special place in my heart that only a father can. I don't know much right now. My surroundings are so different, and there are many uncertainties. But I do know that I love you very much, Daddy.

Love,
Your newborn child

Thanks, Dad...
For Speaking Kindly

LET NO CORRUPT WORD PROCEED OUT OF
YOUR MOUTH, BUT WHAT IS GOOD FOR
NECESSARY EDIFICATION, THAT IT MAY IMPART
GRACE TO THE HEARERS.

EPHESIANS 4:29 NKJV

THE WORDS THAT A FATHER SPEAKS TO HIS
CHILDREN IN THE PRIVACY OF HOME ARE NOT
HEARD BY THE WORLD, BUT, AS IN WHISPERING
GALLERIES, THEY ARE CLEARLY HEARD AT THE
END, AND BY POSTERITY.

JEAN PAUL RICHTER

A GENTLE ANSWER TURNS AWAY WRATH,
BUT A HARSH WORD STIRS UP ANGER.

PROVERBS 15:1 NIV

Thanks, Dad . . .
For Understanding Me

A GRANDFATHER WAS WALKING THROUGH HIS YARD WHEN
HE HEARD HIS GRANDDAUGHTER REPEATING THE ALPHABET
IN A TONE OF VOICE THAT SOUNDED LIKE A PRAYER.
HE ASKED HER WHAT SHE WAS DOING. THE LITTLE GIRL
EXPLAINED: "I'M PRAYING, BUT I CAN'T THINK OF EXACTLY
THE RIGHT WORDS, SO I'M JUST SAYING ALL THE LETTERS,
AND GOD WILL PUT THEM TOGETHER FOR ME, BECAUSE
HE KNOWS WHAT I'M THINKING."

CHARLES B. VAUGHAN

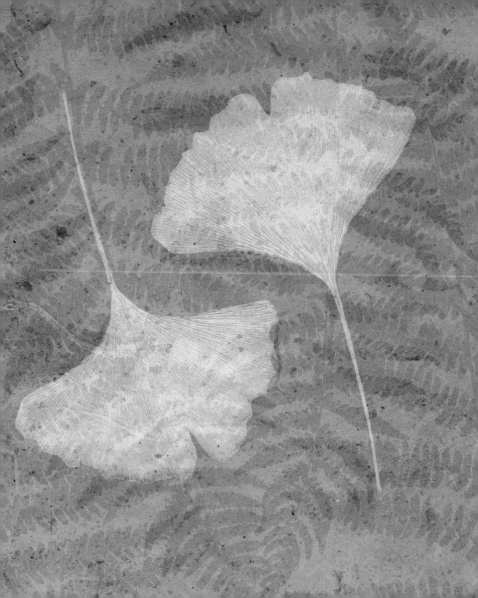

Thanks, Dad...
For Your Gentle Touch

Dads need to color, wrestle, give "horseyback" rides, play that ever popular sport "roll the ball," and even be willing to (at least occasionally) pay some attention to a favorite doll.

MICHAEL FARRIS

GOVERN A FAMILY AS YOU WOULD COOK A SMALL FISH—VERY GENTLY.

CHINESE PROVERB

Dear Daddy,

Thank you for playing with me. I love to giggle when you chase me around and around. And you are really good at making tents, too! I had fun helping you water the plants. I know that I made a big mess, but it made me feel so important to be helping my daddy. Thank you for reading my favorite story to me tonight, and for not leaving any parts out. I really like to hear your voice. I love you, Daddy!

Love,
Your toddler

Thanks, Dad...
For Being an Example of Our Heavenly Father

AS A FATHER HAS COMPASSION ON HIS CHILDREN,
SO THE LORD HAS COMPASSION ON THOSE WHO FEAR HIM.

PSALM 103:13 NIV

Jesus wants us to learn from our experiences of being a father on earth to know the Father in heaven. God is the true Father. His very nature is the God of Love. Fatherhood was the glory and the blessedness of the divine being. Our fatherhood on earth has been given as a reflection of His, and to lead us to a participation in its honor and joy. We, too, are to taste the blessedness of producing a child in our likeness. In him, we will find the object of our love, the reflection of our image, and a companion and helper in all our work.

ANDREW MURRAY,
Raising Your Children for Christ

Thanks, Dad...
For Our Family Traditions

Family traditions that review family history and stimulate
joyful memories of family relationships are an integral part of
building a legacy of joy. Wise fathers look for ways to be deliberate
and creative in reinforcing positive memories. With the fast pace
of life, it becomes especially important to plant solid, positive
memories as valuable building blocks for a future filled with joy.

MIKE NAPPA AND NORM WAKEFIELD,
Legacy of Joy: A Devotional for Fathers

CHILDREN ARE A GIFT FROM THE LORD;
THEY ARE A REWARD FROM HIM.

PSALM 127:3 NLT

Thanks, Dad...
For My Heritage

Even when I am old and gray,
do not forsake me, O God,
till I declare your power to the next generation,
your might to all who are to come.

PSALM 71:18 NIV

Thanks, Dad...
For My Spiritual Training

SHEPHERD THE FLOCK OF GOD WHICH IS AMONG YOU. . .
[NOT] AS BEING LORDS OVER THOSE ENTRUSTED TO YOU,
BUT BEING EXAMPLES TO THE FLOCK.

1 PETER 5:2–3 NKJV

THE PRIMARY LEARNING SYSTEM FOR CHILDREN IS
BY EXAMPLE, AND YOU ARE OFTEN THAT EXAMPLE.

CHRIS EWING

FATHERS, DO NOT EXASPERATE YOUR CHILDREN;
INSTEAD, BRING THEM UP IN THE TRAINING
AND INSTRUCTION OF THE LORD.

EPHESIANS 6:4 NIV

Thanks, Dad...
For Praying for Me

"Give my son Solomon the wholehearted desire
to obey all your commands, decrees,
and principles, and to build this Temple,
for which I have made all these preparations."

1 CHRONICLES 29:19 NLT

"I asked the LORD to give me this child,
and he has given me my request."

1 SAMUEL 1:27 NLT

Our Father in heaven, give us more insight into Your Fatherhood. Help us to see how You command and expect that our fatherhood should be the reflection of Your own. May they indeed be one: one in purpose, one in method, one in principle, one in spirit.

O God, we want to be fathers to our children, just as You are to us. Make us such, so that You can fully use us as the channels for Your grace to our little ones. May they see in us true pictures of Him to whom we teach them to say, Our Father which art in heaven. Father, we look to Your Son for the answer to our prayer. We count upon the tenderness and the faithfulness of Your love and Your mighty power and Spirit to bless the parents of Your Church who pray to You. Amen.

ANDREW MURRAY,
Raising Your Children for Christ

Thanks, Dad...
For Disciplining Me

A FOOL SPURNS HIS FATHER'S DISCIPLINE,
BUT WHOEVER HEEDS CORRECTION SHOWS PRUDENCE.

PROVERBS 15:5 NIV

Children and teenagers need to see a love from parents
that is powerful enough to help them when they need it.
They need a love strong enough to say no.
(Much like God's.)
They need a love that says, "I love you too much
to stand by and watch you hurt yourself."

DAVID MILLER

Dear Daddy,

You're such a cool dad! I do promise that I will feed my new puppy and take him out for walks! Thanks for telling me why you were changing the oil in the car when I asked, and not just saying, "Because." I was happy that you could go to my school program tonight. And then you took us out for ice cream afterward. That was lots of fun! I'm really scared about my recital this weekend. I hope you aren't really sick of hearing the same song over and over again. Thanks for being my dad.

I love you!
Your ten-year-old

*Thanks, Dad...
For Supporting Me*

And a voice from heaven said,
"This is my beloved Son,
and I am fully pleased with him."

MATTHEW 3:17 NLT

Thanks, Dad...
For Your Patience

Patience and forgiveness of minor wrongs or hasty
words are critical traits for parenting and must work
both ways. The important thing to remember is that,
with God's help and support, your family loves you and,
hopefully sooner than later, will come to know that you
have done your best for them.

CHRIS EWING

YOU NEED TO PERSEVERE SO THAT
WHEN YOU HAVE DONE THE WILL OF GOD,
YOU WILL RECEIVE WHAT HE HAS PROMISED.

HEBREWS 10:36 NIV

Thanks, Dad...
For Your Faithfulness

"Well done, good and faithful servant; you were
faithful over a few things, I will make you ruler over
many things. Enter into the joy of your lord."

MATTHEW 25:21 NKJV

"For the eyes of the LORD run to and fro throughout
the whole earth, to show Himself strong on behalf
of those whose heart is loyal to Him."

2 CHRONICLES 16:9 NKJV

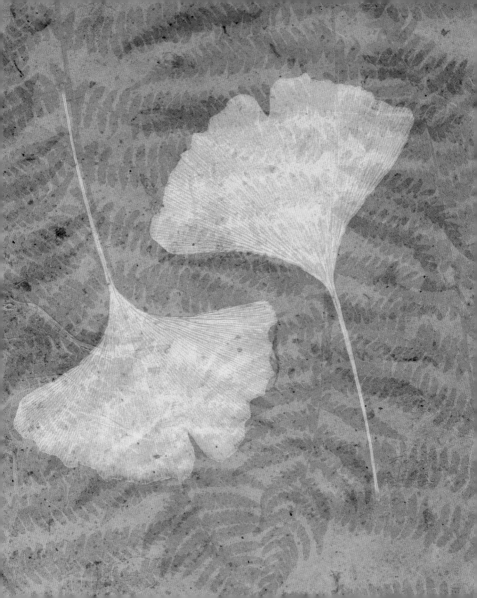

Dear Dad,

Thank you for coming to my soccer game today. I know it was probably hard for you to leave work, but it meant a lot to me. A lot of the kids' dads don't come, and I'm thankful that you take the time to show up and cheer my team and me on.

I really appreciate your time in helping me with my algebra homework. It can get so frustrating, but last night I finally understood after you patiently explained the formula again.

Can we go driving again soon? I know I really scared you last time, but you're a great teacher, and I know that I'll be a good driver with you instructing me.

Dad, thanks for listening when I talk to you. It meant a lot yesterday when you put your newspaper down and gave me your attention. I know my problem probably seems minor to you, but letting me talk about it really helps.

Thanks, Dad! I love you. You're the best!

Love,
Your teenager

Thanks, Dad. . .
For Giving Your Time

One of the many fond memories I have of my father is his recognition of my "half birthday." Because my birthday falls just before Christmas, Dad wanted me to have a special birthday celebration. Annually, in mid-June, he would say, "Be thinking of where you would like to go for your half birthday."

It was always a special time with my father. We would dine at a beautiful restaurant, and then would do something special together after dinner. This was often the ultimate act of fatherly sacrifice—GOING SHOPPING.

For one evening each year, it was established that my father and I would have our own special time. The food and surroundings were always exceptional; however, the thought that he had remembered and planned my special day was—and is—a source of joy. What he did made me feel valued and loved. Thank you, Dad, for such a wonderful birthday gift. . .

THE GIFT OF YOUR TIME.

Thanks, Dad...
For Making Me Feel So Important

What higher form of respect and love
can you demonstrate than to put yourself aside
and give nothing but a few minutes of your attention?

CHRIS EWING

Thanks, Dad...
For Your Leadership

"Choose for yourselves this day
whom you will serve. . . .
But as for me and my household,
we will serve the LORD."

JOSHUA 24:15 NIV

Dear Dad,

How can I begin to thank you for all that you've done for me throughout my life? Your love, support, and sacrifice have helped mold me into the person I am today. Because of your influence in my life, I have accomplished so many things—from earning my college degree to marrying my wonderful mate.

As I think back throughout the years, I realize that I have not thanked you enough for all you have done. Please understand that although it may not have been verbalized, my heart was always full of gratitude for all you did for me. There were many expenses involved for music lessons and extracurricular activities, and much time involved in chauffeuring me to and from those activities. I appreciate all that you did to make it all possible.

Thanks for being appreciative of all of those Father's Day gifts and for actually wearing them. Thank you for the patient instruction in riding bikes, swimming, math, and driving. Thank you for being my supporter at school programs, sporting events, and the biggest day of my life—my wedding day. Thank you for loving Mom. And thank you for being a clear example of our heavenly Father.

THANK YOU, DAD!
I APPRECIATE ALL THAT YOU DO
AND ALL THAT YOU ARE.

I love you.
Your grown child

"Honor your father and mother"—
which is the first commandment with a promise—
"that it may go well with you and
that you may enjoy long life on the earth."

EPHESIANS 6:2–3 NIV

Thanks, Dad !